Book Title:

"Coffee in Daily Life : How Coffee Shapes Our Routines and Social Interactions"

By Jenny Koo

Imprint: Independently published.

Copyright © 2024 by Jenny K. Koo. All rights reserved.

No part of this book may be used or reproduced in any manner whatsoever without written permission.

For information, please email to
jennykookk@gmail.com

"Coffee in Daily Life : How Coffee Shapes Our Routines and Social Interactions "

By Jenny Koo

Table of Contents

Introduction
1. The Ubiquity of Coffee
2. Overview of the Book

Chapter 1: The Morning Ritual
1. Starting the Day with Coffee
2. Personal Rituals
3. Psychological Benefits

Chapter 2: Coffee in the Workplace
1. Coffee Breaks
2. Social Interactions
3. Remote Work and Home Brewing

Chapter 3: Social Aspects of Coffee
1. Coffee Shops as Social Hubs
2. Coffee Dates and Meetings
3. Cultural Significance

Chapter 4: Health and Wellness
1. Caffeine and Alertness
2. Moderation and Health
3. Coffee and Mental Health

Chapter 5: Coffee and Productivity
1. Strategic Coffee Consumption
2. Coffee and Creativity
3. Case Studies

Chapter 6: The Future of Coffee in Daily Life
1. Emerging Trends
2. Technological Innovations
3. Sustainable Practices

Conclusion
1. Recap of Key Points
2. Encouragement to Reflect

Introduction

The Ubiquity of Coffee

Coffee. It's not just a drink; it's a ritual, a comfort, a connection, and for many, a way of life. Whether it's the rich aroma that wafts through the kitchen in the early morning hours or the familiar sound of a barista's steam wand in a bustling café, coffee plays a pivotal role in the rhythm of daily life across the globe.

From the farm to the cup, coffee has traveled an incredible journey to become one of the most consumed beverages in the world. Millions of people start their day with a warm cup of coffee, often before they even speak to another person. For some, it's a necessary jolt of caffeine to jump-start productivity; for others, it's a cherished morning ritual that offers a moment of peace before the busyness of the day begins. But beyond its ability to energize, coffee has seeped into almost every aspect of social life and culture.

Coffee is more than a beverage—it's an experience. In office environments, it's the excuse to take a mental break and socialize with coworkers. In social settings, it fosters conversations, meetings, and dates. And as coffee culture evolves, we see it reflected in trendy cafes, home brewing innovations, and a growing emphasis on sustainable practices. It's a drink that adapts to the needs of both the individual and society, whether through a quick espresso on the go or a slow brew savored over conversation.

This book seeks to explore coffee's profound role in daily life, not just as a drink but as a social catalyst, a workplace productivity tool, and a contributor to personal well-being. Coffee has carved out an essential place in modern routines, and as you'll discover, it's more than just a source of caffeine—it shapes our days, impacts our health, and serves as a conduit for creativity and connection.

Overview of the Book

In *Coffee in Daily Life*, we'll delve deep into the many ways coffee influences not only our routines but also our social interactions and work habits. This book is divided into several chapters, each tackling a different facet of how coffee affects everyday life, from the morning cup to its impact on work culture, social gatherings, health, and even future trends.

In **Chapter 1: The Morning Ritual**, we'll begin by looking at how coffee has become an essential part of the morning routine for so many people. You'll learn how different cultures and individuals celebrate their morning coffee in various ways, and how this simple act can have psychological benefits that provide comfort and routine.

Chapter 2: Coffee in the Workplace will explore how coffee has become a symbol of productivity and camaraderie in professional settings. Whether you work in an office or remotely from home, coffee serves as a necessary break, a chance to recharge, and a way to bond with colleagues.

Next, in **Chapter 3: Social Aspects of Coffee**, we'll explore how coffee transcends the cup to foster social connections. Cafes have become social hubs where people gather to converse, collaborate, or simply relax. From casual coffee dates to professional meetings, we'll examine how coffee has become the backdrop for both personal and professional interactions. We'll also take a look at the cultural significance of coffee in various parts of the world and the unique rituals associated with it.

In **Chapter 4: Health and Wellness**, the book will shift gears to discuss the health implications of coffee consumption. We'll look at its role in boosting alertness and cognitive function, while also examining the importance of moderation and the psychological comfort that coffee can bring to our mental well-being.

Chapter 5: Coffee and Productivity will focus on how coffee is strategically consumed to enhance productivity and creativity. You'll discover how professionals and creatives alike use coffee as a tool to fuel their work and unlock new ideas.

Finally, in **Chapter 6: The Future of Coffee in Daily Life**, we'll explore emerging trends and innovations in the coffee world. From new brewing technologies to the growing movement toward sustainability, we'll consider how the future of coffee will continue to shape our daily routines and impact society as a whole.

By the end of this book, you'll have gained a deeper appreciation for how coffee fits into your life and the lives of others. Whether you're a casual coffee drinker or a seasoned coffee enthusiast, this exploration will offer insights into the trends, rituals, and cultural importance of coffee around the world. More importantly, it will encourage you to reflect on your own coffee habits and consider how this seemingly simple drink contributes to your personal routine and social connections.

So, grab your favorite cup of coffee, settle into a cozy chair, and join me on this journey into the world of coffee—an essential part of daily life for millions, a constant companion in work and play, and an experience worth savoring.

Chapter 1: The Morning Ritual

Starting the Day with Coffee

For millions of people around the world, mornings just don't begin without coffee. It's a ritual that signals the start of a new day, a moment to prepare mentally for what lies ahead. Whether brewed in a quiet kitchen or picked up from a favorite café, coffee serves as both a physical and psychological wake-up call, providing the energy and comfort many need to face the day.

The morning coffee ritual is deeply personal, yet universally recognized. Some take their coffee black, savoring the bold, unadulterated taste of the beans, while others prefer a sweet, milky concoction. The process itself can be as simple or elaborate as one desires—from the quick convenience of a coffee pod machine to the slow, careful craft of a pour-over or French press. Regardless of the method, that first sip holds a special significance.

Culturally, the morning coffee habit varies widely. In Italy, a small but powerful shot of espresso is the norm, while in Sweden, a slower "fika" tradition encourages time for reflection and conversation over coffee and pastries. In the United States, the coffee-to-go culture dominates, with commuters grabbing a cup from a drive-through or a local café as they head to work. Yet, no matter the setting or style, the role of coffee as the day's opener remains a constant.

But why is coffee so intertwined with our morning routines? Part of the answer lies in its ability to kick-start our minds and bodies. Coffee's primary ingredient—caffeine—is a natural stimulant that increases alertness, improves concentration, and even enhances mood. For many, that first cup is less about habit and more about necessity; it helps clear the fog of sleep and provides the mental boost needed to tackle the day.

In addition to its physical effects, coffee also offers psychological comfort. The ritual of making or buying coffee each morning gives structure to the day, offering a familiar and soothing routine that brings calm amidst the chaos of life. It's a brief pause before the rush of responsibilities begins, a moment to gather one's thoughts, reflect, or simply enjoy the quiet.

For some, the act of preparing coffee is almost meditative. The sound of beans grinding, the slow drip of water through a filter, the gentle steam rising from the cup—all of these small details contribute to a sense of mindfulness that helps many people ease into their day. Even in busy households or hectic environments, coffee provides a few precious minutes of focus and reflection.

Personal Rituals

While coffee may be universal, the way people enjoy it varies from person to person. Coffee rituals are as diverse as the people who drink it, with each individual adding their own personal touch to the process.

For some, the ritual begins the night before, with beans carefully measured and equipment set up, ready for the next morning. This small act of preparation transforms the morning coffee from a simple drink into a purposeful, anticipated moment. Others embrace a more spontaneous approach, deciding in the moment whether they'll indulge in a latte, an espresso, or simply a cup of black coffee.

Some coffee drinkers prefer to enjoy their first cup in solitude, using the quiet time to read, journal, or simply reflect on the day ahead. Others make coffee a more social activity, gathering with family members or roommates to chat over a shared pot before everyone heads their separate ways. For those who grab their coffee on the go, the daily trip to the café becomes a social ritual in itself—interacting with the barista, bumping into regulars, and feeling a sense of connection with the community before diving into the demands of the day.

Interestingly, personal coffee rituals also reflect individual priorities and lifestyle choices. Some focus on the quality of the coffee itself, seeking out specialty beans and experimenting with brewing methods to create the perfect cup. Others place more emphasis on convenience, opting for quick and easy methods that fit seamlessly into a busy schedule. In either case, the act of making or enjoying coffee remains an essential part of the morning routine, offering both comfort and energy.

Psychological Benefits

While coffee is celebrated for its physical effects—boosting energy, improving alertness, and enhancing cognitive function—it also has a powerful psychological impact. Beyond being a source of caffeine, coffee holds a unique place in our routines as a ritual that provides comfort, stability, and even a sense of control over the day.

At its core, the morning coffee ritual serves as a mental anchor, creating a moment of calm and predictability. In a world where many aspects of life are unpredictable or chaotic, this small daily habit offers a reassuring sense of normalcy. The simple act of preparing coffee—whether grinding fresh beans, waiting for a machine to brew, or stopping by a familiar café—brings structure to the start of the day. It's a moment that is entirely yours, and for many, it is a time to pause, reflect, and mentally prepare for what lies ahead.

This ritual can be grounding, especially for those with busy, demanding lives. The routine nature of making or consuming coffee helps reduce stress and anxiety, as the familiar process of brewing or sipping coffee can signal to the brain that it's time to shift from rest to productivity. For some, it's less about the caffeine and more about the sense of ritual itself—the warm cup in hand, the aroma of freshly brewed coffee, and the few quiet moments before the day's tasks begin.

Research has shown that rituals, even simple ones like making coffee, can enhance mood and provide emotional comfort. By engaging in these small, consistent habits, we give our brains a mental break, allowing us to focus on something familiar and enjoyable. The psychological benefits of coffee, therefore, go far beyond the chemical boost of caffeine; it becomes an emotional support system woven into the fabric of daily life.

For many, the act of drinking coffee is tied to feelings of relaxation and mindfulness. Sitting down with a cup of coffee allows people to slow down and enjoy the present moment, even if it's just for a few minutes. This pause is often enough to create a sense of mental clarity, reducing the mental clutter that can accompany a busy morning. It's in these moments of quiet that many people find inspiration, make plans for the day, or simply allow themselves to be still.

Moreover, the social aspect of coffee drinking can contribute to a sense of well-being. Whether shared with family, friends, or colleagues, coffee offers a space for connection and conversation. Gathering over a morning cup—whether at the kitchen table, in a café, or virtually over video chat—fosters bonds and provides an opportunity for emotional support. These small, daily interactions can significantly impact mood, offering both companionship and a shared experience in the midst of busy schedules.

In addition, coffee rituals can offer a sense of control, particularly when the rest of the day feels uncertain or overwhelming. For people who face a hectic or unpredictable routine, starting the day with a consistent coffee habit provides a sense of agency. You can control how you make your coffee, how it tastes, and how you enjoy it, which can be especially comforting when the rest of the day feels out of your hands.

This psychological comfort is one of the reasons why so many people fiercely protect their morning coffee rituals. It's more than just a drink; it's a moment of personal time, a grounding ritual, and a way to set a positive tone for the day. Coffee becomes a companion—a reliable part of the morning that is there, day after day, offering both mental clarity and emotional support.

Chapter 2: Coffee in the Workplace

Coffee Breaks: Productivity and Mental Resets

In almost every workplace, whether in a corporate office or a creative studio, coffee plays a central role in the daily routine. From the moment employees walk in, coffee stations buzz with activity as people prepare their first cup to kickstart the workday. But coffee isn't just a beverage consumed for energy—it has woven itself into the fabric of workplace culture, providing essential moments of pause, mental refreshment, and even social bonding.

The concept of the "coffee break" has become a nearly universal practice. Whether it's the mid-morning rush to the office break room or the afternoon walk to a nearby café, these small breaks serve a dual purpose: they provide a much-needed energy boost and offer an opportunity to step away from the work grind. Coffee breaks have become synonymous with productivity, but not in the way one might initially think. While caffeine undoubtedly helps keep employees alert, the value of a coffee break extends far beyond the caffeine hit.

Psychologically, coffee breaks create moments of mental reset. Studies have shown that stepping away from work, even for just a few minutes, improves focus, reduces mental fatigue, and enhances overall productivity. When paired with a cup of coffee, this break becomes a small but powerful ritual—one that allows workers to return to their tasks with renewed energy and clarity. This is why coffee breaks have become ingrained in workplace culture. They signal a time to pause, breathe, and mentally recharge, making them essential for maintaining long-term productivity.

Moreover, these breaks serve as important social moments in the workplace. Coffee breaks naturally bring people together, providing a brief but valuable space for colleagues to connect outside the structure of formal meetings. It's a time for casual conversations, whether about work-related ideas or personal topics, that can strengthen bonds between team members. In many ways, the coffee break serves as a social lubricant in the professional setting, allowing people to communicate more freely and build relationships that enhance collaboration.

The informality of coffee breaks fosters a different kind of interaction. Without the pressures of a formal work setting, colleagues often find themselves brainstorming ideas, offering feedback, or discussing challenges over a cup of coffee. These casual conversations can lead to unexpected insights, creative problem-solving, or new perspectives on work projects. In fact, some of the best ideas in workplaces come not from meetings, but from impromptu coffee chats that allow people to think freely and bounce ideas off one another.

In office environments, these coffee moments have also helped create a sense of community. The shared space around the coffee machine often becomes a hub of interaction, where people from different departments cross paths, share a laugh, or engage in brief, meaningful exchanges. For companies that emphasize open communication and teamwork, coffee breaks have become a vital part of fostering a positive work culture.

But coffee's role in the workplace goes beyond productivity and social interactions. It also supports a sense of ritual in the workday, helping employees structure their time. The predictability of a mid-morning or afternoon coffee break provides a psychological anchor, much like the morning coffee routine at home. For many, the act of taking a coffee break is a way to mark time, creating a natural rhythm in the workday that helps manage stress and maintain focus.

Social Interactions: Coffee as a Networking Tool

Beyond serving as a productivity booster, coffee has taken on an important role in professional networking and relationship-building. The phrase "let's grab a coffee" has become shorthand for informal meetings, whether it's between colleagues, business partners, or even potential clients. Coffee meetings are casual, relaxed, and often more productive than formal settings, allowing conversations to flow naturally and relationships to develop more organically.

In the professional world, coffee meetings are often used as a tool to break the ice and foster connections. The informal nature of these meetings removes the pressure associated with more formal discussions, making it easier for people to open up, share ideas, and build rapport. Whether it's a quick chat about work projects or a deeper discussion about career opportunities, coffee acts as the perfect backdrop for networking. It offers a neutral, relaxed environment where conversations can shift between business and personal topics with ease.

One of the reasons coffee has become such a popular choice for networking is its accessibility. Meeting for coffee doesn't require a large time commitment or significant planning, yet it provides enough time for meaningful conversation. Coffee shops, in particular, have evolved into semi-professional spaces where work and social life intersect. Professionals can meet in a casual, public setting that encourages open dialogue and collaboration, without the formality of a conference room or business lunch.

Moreover, coffee meetings can build connections across hierarchies. In many workplaces, managers and senior leaders use coffee breaks to interact with employees in a more personal and approachable way. These informal coffee chats create opportunities for team members to share ideas, voice concerns, or discuss career goals with leadership. This can break down barriers between levels of management and help cultivate a sense of openness and transparency within the organization.

Remote Work and Home Brewing: Adapting Coffee Rituals

The rise of remote work, accelerated by the global shift during the COVID-19 pandemic, has transformed the way people interact with coffee in their daily work routines. While the office coffee station once served as a social hub and a much-needed mental break, remote workers have had to adapt their coffee rituals to fit their new home-based environments. In doing so, coffee has taken on an even more personalized and crucial role in structuring the workday.

For many remote workers, the transition to working from home blurred the boundaries between personal life and professional responsibilities. The daily commute was replaced with a few steps to the home office, and the once-collaborative environment of a bustling office became a solitary space. In this new dynamic, coffee has evolved from a shared experience to a deeply personal one, offering remote workers a comforting and familiar routine amidst the changes.

One of the first adjustments remote workers made was recreating the coffee breaks they once enjoyed with coworkers. While the social element of in-office coffee breaks may be reduced, the importance of stepping away from work for a coffee pause has only increased. For many, the act of brewing coffee at home offers a much-needed mental reset, a way to mark time and create natural breaks in a day that might otherwise feel unstructured.

Remote workers have also embraced the art of home brewing, which has opened up new possibilities for how they engage with coffee. Freed from the limitations of office coffee machines, remote workers can now experiment with different brewing methods, invest in high-quality beans, and take the time to perfect their morning or afternoon cup. From pour-overs to espresso machines, the home brewing experience allows coffee enthusiasts to craft their coffee exactly the way they like it, transforming a simple break into a more meaningful ritual.

Interestingly, the shift to remote work has also changed how people connect over coffee. While face-to-face coffee chats with coworkers may no longer be a daily occurrence, virtual coffee breaks have become a popular alternative. These informal video calls, often called "coffee catch-ups" or "virtual coffee breaks," provide remote workers with a chance to engage in casual conversation and maintain social bonds with their teams. It's a way to preserve the social aspects of the coffee break, even when everyone is working from different locations.

In these virtual settings, coffee continues to play a vital role in maintaining a sense of normalcy and connection. The act of holding a cup of coffee during a video call can create a shared experience, even when colleagues are miles apart. It allows people to relax, have open conversations, and recreate the atmosphere of an office coffee break in a digital space. This adaptation highlights the enduring importance of coffee as both a personal and social ritual, regardless of where work takes place.

For many remote workers, the coffee break has become more intentional. Rather than rushing through it, they take the time to savor the process of brewing and drinking their coffee, using it as an opportunity to slow down and recharge. In a home office environment where it's easy to blur the lines between work and rest, these coffee moments serve as crucial mental pauses, helping to maintain balance and prevent burnout.

Home brewing has also sparked a growing interest in specialty coffee among remote workers. With the time and freedom to experiment, many have developed a deeper appreciation for the craft of coffee-making. From learning about different brewing methods to exploring single-origin beans, remote workers have turned their home kitchens into mini coffee labs, discovering new ways to enjoy their daily cup. For some, the process of making coffee has become a creative outlet, offering both a mental break and a sensory experience that adds richness to the workday.

Ultimately, coffee's role in the remote work environment has shifted from a purely functional drink to a personal ritual that offers comfort, structure, and connection. Whether through the simple act of brewing a pot at home or sharing a virtual coffee with colleagues, coffee continues to provide moments of pause and reflection, helping remote workers navigate the unique challenges of working from home.

Chapter 3: Social Aspects of Coffee

Coffee Shops as Social Hubs

Coffee shops have evolved into more than just places to grab a quick caffeine fix—they have become central to modern social life. These spaces are the go-to spots for meeting friends, conducting casual business meetings, or simply escaping the hustle and bustle of everyday life for a quiet moment. Whether in a small local café or a bustling chain, coffee shops are social hubs where conversations flow as freely as the coffee.

The ambiance of a coffee shop plays a significant role in fostering connection. With the hum of espresso machines, the soft chatter of customers, and the comforting aroma of freshly brewed coffee, cafés offer an inviting atmosphere that encourages people to linger. It's a space that naturally blends work, relaxation, and social interaction, making it easy to engage with others without the pressure of a formal setting.

In many cities around the world, coffee shops serve as informal gathering spaces. They are the backdrop for everything from casual catch-ups with friends to more intentional, focused conversations. The casual nature of meeting over coffee creates an environment where people can engage in meaningful discussions without the distractions or formalities of other social settings. Whether it's a quick chat or a lengthy conversation, coffee provides a shared experience that encourages connection.

Cafés also serve as communal spaces where people can feel a sense of belonging. Regular customers often develop a relationship with their local baristas, who recognize them by their usual order. Over time, this familiarity can create a sense of community, where both staff and customers contribute to the café's unique social fabric. For many, the local coffee shop becomes a "third place"—a concept popularized by sociologist Ray Oldenburg, referring to the spaces where people gather that aren't home or work. In these third places, people from different walks of life come together, fostering a sense of inclusiveness and community.

The role of coffee shops as social hubs has been especially evident in urban environments, where they provide a welcome respite from the fast-paced rhythm of city life. In these bustling settings, coffee shops offer a sense of calm, a place to sit, relax, and take a break from the hectic surroundings. This duality—being both social and serene—is what makes coffee shops such a popular destination for a wide range of activities, from people-watching to working remotely, all while staying connected to the world around you.

Additionally, cafés have become creative spaces where ideas are born and collaborations take shape. Writers, entrepreneurs, students, and creatives alike flock to coffee shops to work on their projects, drawing inspiration from the energy of the surrounding environment. It's not uncommon to see people huddled over laptops, jotting down ideas in notebooks, or engaging in brainstorming sessions with colleagues over coffee. The balance between solitude and social interaction makes coffee shops ideal for both individual focus and collaborative creativity.

In the digital age, cafés also serve as important networking spaces. With many professionals working remotely or freelancing, coffee shops have become a substitute for traditional office environments. People gather in these spaces not only to work but also to connect with others in their fields. Networking over coffee is informal, but it provides valuable opportunities to build professional relationships in a relaxed setting. Whether it's a chance meeting with someone working on a similar project or a planned meetup with colleagues, the coffee shop has become a key venue for both personal and professional growth.

Moreover, coffee shops often reflect the cultural character of the cities or neighborhoods they inhabit. Local cafés are known for offering more than just coffee—they provide a glimpse into the community's identity. The décor, menu choices, and even the type of coffee served often reflect the values, tastes, and trends of the local area. As such, visiting a coffee shop can be a cultural experience in itself, offering insight into the social and cultural fabric of a community.

From their ability to foster conversation and connection to their role as spaces of creativity and reflection, coffee shops are far more than just places to get a drink. They are integral to modern social life, offering both connection and comfort in an increasingly busy world.

Coffee Dates and Meetings: Facilitating Social Interactions

Coffee has become the drink of choice for social interactions, from casual dates to professional meetings. The simple phrase "let's grab a coffee" has become a ubiquitous way to suggest a low-pressure meeting, whether it's between friends catching up or business associates looking to connect. Coffee's informal nature makes it the perfect companion for a variety of social settings, encouraging open conversation and creating a relaxed atmosphere.

In personal relationships, coffee dates offer a comfortable, no-frills alternative to more formal outings like dinner or drinks. Meeting for coffee feels easy and natural, providing an environment where people can focus on conversation without the distractions or expectations of a more elaborate setting. The neutral nature of a coffee shop or café allows for meaningful interactions, where the drink becomes secondary to the connection between people.

For first-time meetings—whether romantic or platonic—coffee is often the preferred choice. It offers a time-limited, low-commitment setting that takes the pressure off both parties. If the meeting goes well, it can extend naturally with a second cup of coffee or a walk afterward. If not, it's easy to finish the coffee and part ways. This flexibility is one of the reasons why coffee has become such a popular option for meeting new people.

Similarly, in professional settings, coffee meetings offer a relaxed way to build relationships and discuss ideas. Whether it's a job interview, a networking opportunity, or an informal check-in between colleagues, coffee provides a comfortable backdrop for conversation. The setting allows for open dialogue, making it easier to connect on a personal level before diving into business topics.

For many professionals, coffee meetings are an essential networking tool. Unlike formal office meetings, coffee chats offer a chance to talk freely and build rapport in a more casual environment. These meetings are often less about closing deals or making big decisions and more about establishing trust, exchanging ideas, and learning from one another. The casual nature of coffee helps break down barriers, making it easier for people to engage in honest and productive conversations.

Coffee meetings are also ideal for creative discussions, where ideas can be bounced around in a relaxed, free-flowing way. Without the constraints of a formal meeting room, the conversation tends to be more open, leading to more innovative thinking and problem-solving. In fact, many business partnerships, collaborations, and creative projects have been born over a simple cup of coffee.

Cultural Significance: Coffee Rituals Around the World

Coffee is more than just a drink—it's a cultural experience. Across the globe, coffee rituals reflect local customs, values, and social norms, making it a window into the heart of a culture. Each country has its unique relationship with coffee, from the way it's brewed and consumed to the traditions and social interactions that surround it.

In **Italy**, coffee culture is deeply ingrained in daily life. The Italians' approach to coffee is purposeful and efficient. Espresso is the drink of choice, typically consumed quickly while standing at the bar. It's not unusual for Italians to have multiple espressos throughout the day, often without lingering over them for long. The simplicity of the espresso mirrors the fast-paced nature of Italian cities like Rome and Milan, where coffee breaks are brief but essential moments of refreshment. Interestingly, milk-based coffees like cappuccinos are reserved for mornings only—ordering one after lunch or dinner is considered a faux pas in traditional Italian culture.

Ethiopia, widely regarded as the birthplace of coffee, celebrates coffee with a rich and elaborate ritual. The Ethiopian coffee ceremony is a cornerstone of the country's social and cultural life. It's a slow, deliberate process that can take hours and involves roasting green coffee beans, grinding them by hand, and brewing the coffee in a special pot called a *jebena*. The ceremony is as much about the social interaction as it is about the coffee itself. Family and friends gather to share stories and connect over multiple rounds of coffee, which is traditionally served with popcorn or other snacks. In Ethiopia, coffee isn't just a beverage—it's a symbol of hospitality and community.

In **Sweden**, coffee drinking is elevated to a social institution known as *fika*. More than just a coffee break, *fika* is a cherished ritual of taking time to pause and enjoy a cup of coffee with friends, colleagues, or family, often accompanied by pastries or small snacks. The emphasis is on slowing down and making time for conversation, creating a space for relaxation and connection. In Swedish culture, *fika* isn't just an optional break—it's considered an important part of the day, a moment to reset and recharge while strengthening relationships.

Turkey also has a rich coffee tradition that dates back centuries. Turkish coffee is thick, strong, and unfiltered, with fine coffee grounds settling at the bottom of the cup. The preparation of Turkish coffee is often a ceremonial process, particularly during special occasions like weddings or family gatherings. Turkish coffee culture extends beyond drinking—there's a tradition of reading fortunes from the coffee grounds left in the cup, adding a mystical element to the experience. In Turkey, coffee is often shared in small, intimate settings, symbolizing friendship and hospitality.

In the **Middle East**, coffee is deeply intertwined with hospitality. Arabic coffee, known as *gahwa*, is served in small cups and often flavored with spices like cardamom. It's customary for hosts to offer coffee to guests as a sign of generosity and respect. The serving of coffee follows a specific etiquette, with the youngest person typically serving the eldest first, highlighting the importance of respect and social hierarchy in Arab culture. Coffee plays a central role in gatherings and celebrations, where it's enjoyed slowly, fostering conversation and community.

In **Latin America**, particularly in countries like **Colombia** and **Brazil**, coffee is both an economic lifeblood and a cultural treasure. As two of the world's largest coffee producers, these countries have a strong connection to coffee farming, which influences the way coffee is appreciated locally. In Colombia, the traditional drink of choice is *tinto*, a small cup of black coffee often sweetened with sugar. Coffee drinking is a social activity, often enjoyed in the afternoon or evening with friends and family. In Brazil, coffee is consumed throughout the day, with *cafézinho*, a small cup of strong, black coffee, being a staple in both homes and offices. Coffee is seen as a gesture of hospitality, and it's not uncommon for visitors to be offered a cup of *cafézinho* as soon as they enter someone's home.

In **Japan**, coffee culture has taken on a distinct form, blending traditional Japanese aesthetics with modern coffee trends. Japan is known for its precision and attention to detail, and this is reflected in the way coffee is brewed and consumed. The art of pour-over brewing, in particular, has gained popularity in Japan, with baristas focusing on every detail of the brewing process to create a perfectly balanced cup of coffee. Japanese coffee shops, or *kissaten*, offer a quiet, contemplative space for enjoying coffee, often paired with a delicate pastry or sweet. The minimalist, refined approach to coffee reflects Japan's broader cultural values of harmony, precision, and mindfulness.

Across these diverse coffee traditions, one thing remains constant: coffee is more than just a drink. It serves as a cultural touchstone, a way of bringing people together, and a reflection of the values and social customs of each society. Whether it's the quick shot of espresso in Italy, the communal coffee ceremony in Ethiopia, or the relaxed *fika* in Sweden, coffee rituals offer a glimpse into how different cultures connect, communicate, and build relationships.

Chapter 4: Health and Wellness

Caffeine and Alertness: The Cognitive Boost

One of the primary reasons people reach for coffee, especially in the morning, is the caffeine boost it provides. Caffeine, the natural stimulant found in coffee, has been shown to improve alertness, concentration, and overall cognitive function, making it an indispensable tool for many in navigating the demands of the day.

Caffeine works by blocking the effects of adenosine, a neurotransmitter in the brain that promotes sleep and relaxation. As adenosine levels rise throughout the day, the brain starts to feel tired and ready for rest. Caffeine interrupts this process by binding to adenosine receptors, preventing the sleep-inducing signal from taking effect and giving the brain a temporary lift in energy and focus.

For most people, the effects of caffeine kick in within 20 minutes of consuming a cup of coffee. This sharp increase in alertness helps shake off the morning grogginess or the mid-afternoon slump, allowing people to perform mental tasks more efficiently. Studies show that moderate caffeine consumption improves attention, reaction times, and memory, especially when someone is tired or sleep-deprived.

But beyond the quick jolt of energy, caffeine's effects are more complex. It can enhance mood, improve motivation, and even foster better decision-making. These benefits explain why coffee is such a popular beverage in workplaces and why it's often the first thing people reach for when they need to focus.

For students and professionals alike, coffee has become a go-to tool for increasing cognitive performance. Whether preparing for an exam, focusing on a project, or solving complex problems at work, caffeine helps boost the brain's ability to process information and stay sharp over extended periods. It's particularly useful in tasks that require sustained attention, such as reading, writing, or managing long meetings.

However, the relationship between caffeine and cognitive performance is not always straightforward. While small to moderate amounts of caffeine can improve mental clarity, consuming too much can lead to negative side effects like jitteriness, anxiety, and difficulty sleeping. For most people, the key to enjoying the cognitive benefits of coffee without experiencing the downsides is moderation.

Moderation and Health: Finding the Balance

While coffee offers many health benefits, particularly when it comes to cognitive function and alertness, the key to maximizing these benefits lies in finding the right balance. As with any stimulant, excessive consumption can have adverse effects on both the body and mind, leading to jitteriness, increased heart rate, and disrupted sleep patterns.

The recommended daily intake of caffeine for most adults is about 400 milligrams, roughly equivalent to four 8-ounce cups of brewed coffee. While this amount is considered safe for the majority of people, individual tolerance to caffeine can vary significantly. Some people are more sensitive to caffeine and may experience symptoms like restlessness, nervousness, or an elevated heart rate even after a single cup, while others can tolerate higher amounts without noticeable effects.

Understanding personal tolerance is crucial to reaping the health benefits of coffee while avoiding potential risks. For those sensitive to caffeine, it might be beneficial to limit intake to one or two cups per day or switch to decaffeinated options in the afternoon to prevent sleep disturbances. Sleep, after all, is one of the most important factors for maintaining overall health, and too much caffeine, especially late in the day, can interfere with the ability to fall asleep or stay asleep.

On the flip side, moderate coffee consumption has been linked to a wide range of health benefits. Numerous studies have shown that drinking coffee in moderation may reduce the risk of several chronic diseases, including type 2 diabetes, Parkinson's disease, and certain types of cancer. Coffee is rich in antioxidants, which help protect cells from damage caused by free radicals—unstable molecules that can contribute to inflammation and the development of chronic illnesses.

Moreover, coffee has been shown to have positive effects on heart health. Recent research suggests that moderate coffee consumption may lower the risk of heart disease and stroke by improving blood vessel function and reducing inflammation. However, these benefits are most pronounced when coffee is consumed in moderate amounts. Drinking excessive amounts, particularly in people who are sensitive to caffeine or have existing heart conditions, can lead to increased blood pressure and heart palpitations.

In addition to its physical benefits, coffee can also have a positive impact on mental health. For many people, the simple act of brewing and drinking coffee provides a sense of comfort and routine that can reduce stress and anxiety. The social aspect of coffee drinking— whether it's sharing a cup with a friend or taking a break with colleagues—also contributes to feelings of connection and well-being.

Still, the conversation around coffee and health is not without its complexities. While coffee has many benefits, it's important to be mindful of how it's consumed. For example, many people enjoy adding sugar, cream, or flavored syrups to their coffee, which can significantly increase calorie intake. Over time, these additions can contribute to weight gain and other health issues, so it's essential to be aware of what goes into your cup.

To strike a balance between enjoying coffee and maintaining good health, experts recommend keeping coffee simple. Black coffee, with minimal or no added sugars or fats, is the healthiest option. If you prefer a bit of sweetness or creaminess, consider healthier alternatives like plant-based milk or natural sweeteners like stevia or honey.

Coffee and Mental Health: The Comfort of Ritual

Coffee does more than just wake us up—it provides a sense of comfort and stability, especially during stressful or busy times. For many, the daily ritual of making or drinking coffee is an important mental break that offers a moment of calm and reflection. This routine can be especially grounding, giving people a way to pause and collect their thoughts before diving into the day's tasks.

In modern life, where stress and anxiety are common, small routines like the coffee break can be powerful tools for mental health. The act of brewing coffee, whether at home or in the office, allows people to engage in a familiar and soothing process that can help alleviate feelings of overwhelm. The repetitive nature of these rituals provides a sense of control and predictability, which is especially valuable when other parts of life feel uncertain or chaotic.

For some, the comfort of coffee is also linked to its social aspects. Sharing a cup with a friend or colleague can strengthen relationships and offer emotional support. In this way, coffee becomes more than just a drink—it becomes a bridge for connection, helping people build and maintain social bonds that are crucial for mental well-being.

Chapter 5: Coffee and Productivity

Strategic Coffee Consumption: Timing for Maximum Effect

For many, coffee is the ultimate tool for boosting productivity. Whether starting the day with a morning cup or reaching for an afternoon pick-me-up, coffee has become a key ally in managing energy levels and improving focus throughout the workday. But like any tool, the effectiveness of coffee depends on how and when it's used. Strategic coffee consumption—timing your coffee intake for maximum productivity—can make a significant difference in how efficiently you work and how energized you feel.

The body's natural energy rhythms play a crucial role in determining when coffee will have the most significant impact. The human body operates on a biological clock known as the circadian rhythm, which regulates various functions, including sleep and wakefulness, energy levels, and hormone release. Throughout the day, the body naturally experiences peaks and dips in alertness. For example, cortisol, a hormone that helps regulate energy, typically peaks in the morning (around 8–9 a.m.) and again in the early afternoon (around 12–1 p.m.).

Drinking coffee during times when cortisol is already high may not be the most efficient use of caffeine. When cortisol levels peak, the body is already in a state of heightened alertness, meaning the additional caffeine may have less noticeable effects or contribute to overstimulation, leading to jitteriness or anxiety. To get the most out of coffee, it's better to time consumption during natural dips in energy—often late morning (around 9:30–11:30 a.m.) and mid-afternoon (around 2–4 p.m.) when cortisol levels decrease, and mental fatigue starts to set in.

By drinking coffee during these dips, caffeine works in synergy with the body's natural rhythms, providing a boost when it's needed most. This timing helps extend periods of focus and productivity, preventing the usual slumps that occur during these times of day. For those who need sustained concentration, such as during a long work meeting or while tackling a demanding project, strategically timed coffee can provide a much-needed second wind without the risk of disrupting sleep patterns later in the day.

It's also important to recognize that not all coffee consumption needs to happen in large quantities. Small, regular doses of caffeine—often called "caffeine microdosing"—can help maintain consistent energy and focus without the crashes that sometimes follow larger cups of coffee. Instead of drinking a large cup of coffee all at once, microdosing involves drinking smaller amounts of coffee or other caffeinated beverages (like tea) throughout the day. This method keeps caffeine levels more stable, preventing the rollercoaster of energy highs and lows that can make it harder to maintain productivity.

For many professionals, particularly those in high-pressure roles that require sustained concentration, caffeine microdosing can help maintain mental clarity over extended periods. By avoiding the energy spikes and crashes, this approach ensures that focus and alertness remain steady throughout the workday.

However, it's also essential to recognize individual tolerance and sensitivity to caffeine. Some people metabolize caffeine more quickly than others, meaning they can drink coffee later in the day without it affecting their sleep. Others may find that even a small amount of caffeine after 2 p.m. can interfere with their ability to wind down at night. Understanding how your body responds to caffeine is key to optimizing your coffee consumption for productivity.

Coffee and Creativity: Fuel for Innovation

Beyond productivity and focus, coffee has long been associated with creativity and innovation. Throughout history, coffee has been the fuel behind countless creative endeavors, from artistic masterpieces to groundbreaking inventions. Whether consumed in solitude by writers and artists or in social settings by entrepreneurs and thinkers, coffee is often credited with sparking new ideas and inspiring creative breakthroughs.

There's a reason why so many creatives gravitate toward coffee. Caffeine's ability to increase alertness and focus can help remove mental blocks and encourage out-of-the-box thinking. When people are more focused and awake, they're better equipped to make connections between ideas that might not seem obvious at first glance. This cognitive flexibility—the ability to shift perspectives and think in new ways—is crucial for creativity, and caffeine has been shown to enhance it.

Interestingly, the social aspect of coffee drinking also plays a role in fostering creativity. Many famous thinkers and innovators, from the writers of the Enlightenment to the tech entrepreneurs of Silicon Valley, have gathered in coffeehouses to share ideas and collaborate. These environments encourage open conversation and the free flow of ideas, making coffee shops the perfect breeding ground for innovation. In these spaces, the combination of caffeine-fueled alertness and the stimulation of exchanging ideas with others can lead to new perspectives and creative breakthroughs.

For those in creative fields, coffee can serve as a reliable companion during the brainstorming process. Whether it's helping to structure a novel, design a new product, or solve a complex problem, coffee can help sharpen focus and stimulate new ideas. Many creatives use coffee not just to fuel long hours of work but as a way to enter a state of "flow," where they're fully immersed in their creative process.

In addition to its effects on focus and creativity, coffee has a stimulating impact on mood. When people feel more positive and energized, they're more likely to approach creative challenges with an open mind. This boost in mood, combined with caffeine's cognitive benefits, creates an ideal mental state for exploring new ideas and taking creative risks. It's no wonder that coffee has been an essential part of creative rituals for centuries.

Case Studies: How Professionals Use Coffee to Enhance Their Work

Coffee is not only a staple for individuals working in traditional office environments but also for professionals across a wide range of fields, from artists and writers to scientists and entrepreneurs. Each of these groups uses coffee strategically, tailoring its consumption to maximize focus, productivity, and creativity. Let's take a closer look at how different professionals leverage coffee as a tool to enhance their work.

1. Writers and Authors: Coffee as a Creative Companion

Writers, perhaps more than any other creative group, are closely associated with coffee. Whether it's the image of an author tapping away at a laptop in a café or a novelist sipping from a cup in a quiet home office, coffee has long been intertwined with the creative writing process.

One famous example is **Honoré de Balzac**, a prolific 19th-century French novelist who credited coffee with helping him write more than 90 novels. Balzac reportedly drank up to 50 cups of coffee per day and often consumed it in concentrated doses to sustain his marathon writing sessions. Though extreme by today's standards, his reliance on coffee highlights how it can be used to maintain focus and drive during long hours of intense creative work.

In modern times, authors like **Haruki Murakami** have written about their daily routines, which often include coffee as an essential part of their creative process. Murakami begins his writing day at 4 a.m., typically with a cup of coffee, noting that the quiet early morning hours and the caffeine boost help him enter a deep creative flow. For writers, coffee is not just a stimulant—it becomes a part of the ritual that sparks creativity and helps them push through long periods of solitary work.

2. Entrepreneurs and Startups: Coffee as Fuel for Innovation

Entrepreneurs and startup founders often credit coffee with powering the long hours and intense focus required to build a business. Coffee plays a pivotal role in startup culture, where late nights and early mornings are the norm. The connection between coffee and innovation is perhaps best exemplified by the **coffeehouses of 17th-century London**, which were known as "penny universities." These coffeehouses became gathering places for intellectuals, merchants, and entrepreneurs, where ideas were shared, deals were made, and new businesses were born.

In today's startup world, coffee continues to serve as the fuel behind innovation. In Silicon Valley, coffee shops are unofficial meeting spaces where tech entrepreneurs and venture capitalists gather to discuss new ideas and forge partnerships. Coffee not only energizes individuals but also serves as a social connector, bringing people together to share knowledge and collaborate on creative solutions.

One famous example is **Howard Schultz**, the CEO of Starbucks, who transformed the American coffee industry by introducing the concept of European-style coffeehouses as "third places"—spaces that are not home or work but somewhere in between, where people can gather, work, and innovate. Schultz's vision for Starbucks grew out of his own love of coffee and his belief in its power to foster creativity and connection.

3. Tech Professionals: Coffee as a Focus Enhancer

For tech professionals, especially those working in coding, development, or data science, coffee is often the key to maintaining focus during long hours of complex, detail-oriented work. Coding requires deep concentration and problem-solving skills, and many developers turn to coffee to help them stay sharp as they work through difficult algorithms and debugging processes.

For instance, **Linus Torvalds**, the creator of Linux, has spoken about his reliance on coffee during the early days of developing the open-source operating system. Coffee helped him stay focused and motivated during intense coding sessions, allowing him to work through challenging problems without mental fatigue.

In the tech world, coffee is also part of the communal culture. Many tech companies, particularly startups, offer free, high-quality coffee in their offices, recognizing that it helps employees stay alert and productive. In fact, some tech companies have embraced "coffee culture" to the extent that they install advanced espresso machines or hire in-house baristas to ensure that their teams are fueled by the best coffee available.

4. Scientists and Researchers: Coffee as Cognitive Support

Scientific research is another field where coffee plays a crucial role, especially in laboratory settings where experiments often require long hours of focus and attention to detail. Scientists often use coffee to stay alert during periods of high cognitive demand, whether they're conducting experiments, analyzing data, or writing research papers.

One example is **Charles Darwin**, who was known for his meticulous approach to scientific inquiry. Though primarily a tea drinker, Darwin often turned to coffee during intense periods of work, particularly while drafting his groundbreaking work, *On the Origin of Species*. Like many scientists, Darwin found that coffee helped him sustain focus and energy during long hours of writing and experimentation.

In modern research environments, coffee serves as both a cognitive aid and a social bridge. In many labs and universities, coffee breaks are an essential part of the workday, providing researchers with the chance to step away from their work, recharge, and exchange ideas with colleagues. These informal interactions over coffee often lead to new insights and collaborative opportunities, making coffee an integral part of the scientific process.

5. Artists and Creatives: Coffee as a Source of Inspiration

Artists, from painters to designers, have long used coffee to fuel their creative output. For many, the act of drinking coffee serves as a ritual that helps them enter a creative state of mind. The repetitive nature of preparing coffee can be meditative, allowing artists to clear their minds and focus on their work.

One notable example is the surrealist artist **Salvador Dalí**, who often incorporated coffee into his daily routine. While Dalí was known for his eccentric habits, coffee was a staple that helped him maintain energy and focus during his long hours of painting. Similarly, modern artists and designers use coffee to stimulate creativity, often pairing it with sketching or brainstorming sessions to unlock new ideas.

Coffee's ability to sharpen focus and enhance mood makes it an ideal companion for artists working on complex projects. Whether working alone in a studio or collaborating in a design workshop, coffee helps artists sustain their creative energy over time, making it a crucial tool in the artistic process.

Chapter 6: The Future of Coffee in Daily Life

Emerging Trends: New Ways Coffee is Being Integrated into Daily Routines

As coffee continues to be a beloved part of daily life, its consumption is evolving, reflecting shifts in culture, technology, and environmental consciousness. Coffee drinkers are no longer content with just a basic cup of joe; they're seeking new experiences, flavors, and methods of preparation. As a result, coffee culture is constantly adapting, with several emerging trends shaping the future of how people engage with this iconic beverage.

1. Cold Brew and Nitro Coffee: The Rise of Iced Coffee Innovations

In recent years, cold brew coffee has skyrocketed in popularity, offering a smoother, less acidic alternative to traditional iced coffee. Unlike hot-brewed coffee, which is cooled down with ice, cold brew is made by steeping coffee grounds in cold water for 12 to 24 hours. This slow extraction process creates a rich, concentrated flavor that has won over a new generation of coffee drinkers, particularly during warmer months.

In addition to cold brew, **nitro coffee**—infused with nitrogen gas—has gained traction, especially among those seeking a more indulgent coffee experience. Nitro coffee has a creamy texture and a velvety head similar to that of a stout beer, giving it a luxurious feel without the need for added cream or sugar. The combination of cold brew and nitro innovations reflects a broader shift toward iced coffee drinks that offer both convenience and sophistication.

2. Specialty Coffee and Single-Origin Beans: A Focus on Quality

As consumers become more knowledgeable about coffee, there's been a growing demand for high-quality, specialty coffee. Specialty coffee refers to beans that are graded at 80 or above on a 100-point scale, representing the best of the best in terms of flavor, aroma, and overall quality. These beans are often sourced from specific regions or even individual farms, allowing consumers to experience the unique characteristics of different coffee-growing environments.

Single-origin coffee—beans sourced from one specific location—is particularly popular among coffee aficionados who enjoy exploring the diverse flavors that come from different parts of the world. For example, coffee from Ethiopia may have fruity and floral notes, while beans from Colombia might offer a more balanced, nutty flavor. This focus on origin and quality reflects a growing appreciation for the craft behind coffee production and a desire for transparency about where coffee comes from and how it's made.

As more consumers seek out specialty and single-origin coffees, there's a greater emphasis on traceability and sustainability. Coffee drinkers want to know the story behind their cup—who grew the beans, how they were processed, and what impact their purchase has on the environment and coffee-growing communities. This shift toward conscious consumption is shaping the future of coffee, with more roasters and brands highlighting the ethical and sustainable practices behind their products.

3. Plant-Based Milk Alternatives: A Move Toward Sustainability

The rise of plant-based diets and the growing awareness of environmental issues have significantly impacted coffee culture, particularly when it comes to milk and cream alternatives. Traditional dairy milk has long been a staple in lattes, cappuccinos, and macchiatos, but in recent years, plant-based options like almond, soy, oat, and coconut milk have become increasingly popular.

For many, these alternatives aren't just about dietary preferences—they're a way to reduce their environmental footprint. Dairy farming is known to have a higher environmental impact than plant-based agriculture, requiring more water and contributing more to greenhouse gas emissions. By switching to plant-based milk, coffee drinkers are making choices that align with a more sustainable lifestyle.

Oat milk, in particular, has surged in popularity due to its creamy texture and neutral flavor, which complements coffee without overpowering it. Baristas have also embraced oat milk for its ability to froth similarly to cow's milk, making it a perfect option for lattes and cappuccinos. As plant-based alternatives continue to improve in both flavor and texture, they are becoming a permanent fixture in coffee culture, allowing more people to enjoy their favorite coffee drinks while making environmentally conscious choices.

Technological Innovations: How Technology is Changing Coffee Consumption

As technology continues to revolutionize various aspects of daily life, coffee is no exception. From brewing methods to mobile apps, technological innovations are transforming how people buy, brew, and enjoy coffee. In particular, technology has made it easier to personalize the coffee experience, offering consumers more control over everything from the grind size of their beans to the temperature of their brew.

1. Smart Coffee Machines: Precision Brewing at Home

One of the most significant technological advances in coffee is the rise of **smart coffee machines**. These devices allow users to brew their coffee with precision, often controlled via smartphone apps. With features like temperature control, grind size adjustments, and brewing time customization, smart coffee makers enable people to replicate the café experience from the comfort of their homes.

Some smart coffee machines even come equipped with built-in grinders, allowing users to grind fresh beans right before brewing, which can significantly enhance the flavor of the coffee. These machines are designed for coffee enthusiasts who want full control over the brewing process, ensuring that each cup is perfectly tailored to their preferences.

In addition, many of these devices are integrated with voice-activated systems like **Amazon Alexa** or **Google Assistant**, allowing users to start their coffee brewing process through simple voice commands. This integration makes it easier than ever for coffee lovers to brew their perfect cup without lifting a finger—ideal for busy mornings when every minute counts.

2. Mobile Apps and Subscriptions: The Convenience of Coffee on Demand

Mobile technology has also reshaped how people access and enjoy coffee. Coffeehouse chains and independent cafés alike have adopted mobile apps that allow customers to order and pay for their coffee ahead of time, reducing wait times and enhancing convenience. Apps from companies like **Starbucks** and **Dunkin'** have made it possible for people to customize their orders down to the smallest detail and pick up their drinks with minimal interaction, a particularly valuable feature during the COVID-19 pandemic.

Subscription services have also become a growing trend in the coffee industry. Companies now offer monthly coffee subscription boxes that deliver freshly roasted beans directly to customers' doors. These services often allow consumers to explore a wide range of coffees, from rare single-origin beans to exclusive blends from top roasters. The convenience of having fresh coffee delivered regularly appeals to busy professionals and coffee enthusiasts who want to explore new flavors without leaving home.

Moreover, these services often come with an educational component, providing information about the origin of the beans, tasting notes, and brewing tips. For coffee lovers who want to deepen their knowledge and appreciation of coffee, these subscriptions offer an immersive experience that goes beyond just the drink.

Sustainable Practices: The Role of Eco-Friendly Coffee in Daily Life

As global awareness of climate change and environmental sustainability grows, the coffee industry is under increasing pressure to adopt more eco-friendly practices. From the way coffee is farmed to how it's packaged and consumed, sustainability is becoming a major factor influencing consumer choices. The future of coffee is not only about creating better brews but also about ensuring that the process behind each cup is environmentally responsible and ethical.

1. Fair Trade and Direct Trade: Supporting Farmers and Ethical Practices

One of the biggest challenges in the coffee industry is ensuring that coffee farmers, many of whom live in developing countries, are fairly compensated for their work. Historically, coffee farming has been associated with low wages and poor working conditions, but initiatives like **Fair Trade** and **Direct Trade** aim to change that by creating more equitable and sustainable supply chains.

Fair Trade coffee ensures that farmers receive a fair price for their beans, which helps improve their living conditions and allows them to invest in sustainable farming practices. By paying farmers a premium, Fair Trade encourages environmentally friendly methods such as organic farming and biodiversity preservation. Consumers who choose Fair Trade coffee are supporting both ethical labor practices and environmental sustainability, making it a win-win for everyone involved.

Direct Trade takes this a step further by fostering direct relationships between coffee roasters and farmers, cutting out middlemen to ensure that more of the profits go directly to the producers. This method allows for greater transparency in the supply chain, ensuring that the coffee is not only ethically sourced but also of higher quality. Roasters often visit farms to ensure that sustainable practices are in place and to establish long-term relationships with farmers, which can lead to more consistent and higher-quality coffee.

These practices reflect a growing consumer desire to know where their coffee comes from and to support brands that prioritize ethical sourcing. As consumers become more conscious of the impact of their purchases, the demand for Fair Trade and Direct Trade coffee is expected to rise, driving the industry toward more sustainable and socially responsible practices.

2. Organic and Shade-Grown Coffee: Protecting Ecosystems

Sustainable coffee production goes beyond just fair wages and ethical sourcing—it's also about minimizing the environmental impact of farming. **Organic coffee** is grown without synthetic fertilizers, pesticides, or genetically modified organisms (GMOs), making it a healthier choice for both consumers and the environment. Organic farming practices help preserve soil health, protect water supplies from contamination, and reduce the overall carbon footprint of coffee production.

Another eco-friendly method is **shade-grown coffee**, where coffee plants are cultivated under the canopy of trees, mimicking the coffee plant's natural growing environment. This method not only reduces the need for chemical inputs but also helps maintain biodiversity by providing a habitat for birds, insects, and other wildlife. Shade-grown coffee farms are also better at conserving water and preventing soil erosion compared to sun-grown coffee plantations, which often require deforestation and lead to habitat destruction.

By choosing organic and shade-grown coffee, consumers can support farming practices that protect ecosystems and promote long-term sustainability. As environmental concerns continue to shape consumer habits, the demand for eco-friendly coffee options is likely to grow, encouraging more farms to adopt sustainable agricultural methods.

3. Compostable and Reusable Packaging: Reducing Waste

The shift toward sustainability is not limited to how coffee is grown—it extends to how it's packaged and consumed. Traditional coffee packaging, especially single-use plastic and aluminum capsules, contributes significantly to global waste. As environmental awareness grows, companies are seeking more sustainable alternatives to reduce their environmental impact.

One popular solution is **compostable coffee pods**. Unlike traditional plastic or aluminum capsules, compostable pods break down naturally in industrial composting facilities, reducing the amount of waste that ends up in landfills. These eco-friendly pods are designed to be used in popular single-serve coffee machines, offering the same convenience without the environmental cost. Brands like **Nespresso** and

Keurig have already begun offering compostable options, signaling a larger industry shift toward sustainability.

Another growing trend is the use of **reusable coffee cups and containers**. As consumers become more conscious of waste, many coffee shops have introduced incentives for customers who bring their own reusable cups. Major chains like **Starbucks** and **Costa Coffee** have adopted policies that reward customers with discounts for using their own mugs, reducing the demand for disposable cups and lids, which are often difficult to recycle due to their plastic lining.

For home brewers, **reusable coffee filters** made from stainless steel or cloth are becoming more popular as alternatives to single-use paper filters. These options not only reduce waste but also save money over time, offering an eco-friendly and cost-effective way to enjoy coffee.

4. Carbon-Neutral Coffee: Offsetting Environmental Impact

One of the most ambitious movements within the coffee industry is the push toward **carbon-neutral coffee**. Producing coffee, from farming to shipping and roasting, generates significant carbon emissions, contributing to global warming. To address this issue, some coffee companies are taking steps to reduce their carbon footprint by investing in sustainable farming practices, energy-efficient production methods, and carbon offset programs.

Carbon-neutral coffee brands work to reduce emissions at every stage of production and distribution. For example, they may use renewable energy sources in their roasting facilities, reduce transportation emissions through more efficient logistics, or plant trees to offset the carbon footprint of their operations. By supporting carbon-neutral coffee brands, consumers can enjoy their favorite beverage knowing that steps are being taken to mitigate its environmental impact.

Some companies, like **Counter Culture Coffee** and **Intelligentsia**, have committed to becoming carbon neutral by implementing strategies such as improving energy efficiency and investing in renewable energy sources. These efforts reflect a growing awareness of the need for the coffee industry to address its environmental impact and provide consumers with more sustainable choices.

Conclusion: The Future of Coffee in Our Hands

As coffee continues to play a central role in daily life, it's clear that the future of this beloved beverage will be shaped by emerging trends, technological innovations, and a commitment to sustainability. From the rise of cold brew and plant-based alternatives to the adoption of smart brewing technologies and compostable packaging, coffee culture is evolving to meet the needs of a more conscious and connected world.

At the same time, the future of coffee depends on the choices made by consumers, producers, and companies alike. By supporting ethical sourcing practices, embracing sustainable packaging, and choosing eco-friendly brewing methods, coffee lovers can help ensure that this cherished drink remains not only a source of enjoyment but also a force for positive change.

Ultimately, the future of coffee is in our hands. Whether we're sipping an espresso at a café, brewing a cup of specialty coffee at home, or exploring new innovations in the coffee industry, each decision we make has the power to shape the way coffee is grown, shared, and appreciated for generations to come.

Conclusion

Recap of Key Points

Coffee is far more than just a beverage—it's a ritual, a social connector, a tool for productivity, and a reflection of global cultures. Throughout this book, we've explored the many facets of coffee's role in daily life, from the first cup that kickstarts the morning to the countless social and professional interactions it fosters throughout the day.

In **Chapter 1**, we looked at the morning ritual, discovering how coffee plays a vital role in preparing people mentally and physically for the day ahead. The simple act of brewing or drinking coffee in the morning offers comfort and a sense of control over the day, while also delivering the caffeine boost needed to focus and stay alert.

In **Chapter 2**, we explored coffee in the workplace, where coffee breaks are essential for productivity and mental resets. We also saw how coffee facilitates informal networking and professional connections, making it more than just a source of energy—it's a social and collaborative tool that strengthens team dynamics and sparks creativity.

In **Chapter 3**, we dove into the social aspects of coffee, recognizing how cafés have become social hubs and how coffee plays a central role in fostering personal and professional relationships. We also traveled around the world to learn about diverse coffee rituals that reflect the unique cultural significance of this drink in different regions.

Chapter 4 focused on the health and wellness benefits of coffee. We examined the scientific evidence behind coffee's ability to improve alertness and cognitive function, while also discussing the importance of moderation to ensure that the benefits of coffee are balanced with its potential health risks.

In **Chapter 5**, we explored coffee's impact on productivity and creativity. From its strategic use to enhance focus during critical work hours to its role in fueling innovation, coffee has proven to be an essential tool for professionals across various fields. Case studies of writers, entrepreneurs, and scientists demonstrated how coffee has been used to unlock new ideas and drive productivity.

Finally, in **Chapter 6**, we looked to the future of coffee. Emerging trends like cold brew and nitro coffee, plant-based alternatives, and technological innovations in brewing are shaping the way people enjoy coffee today. We also explored the growing emphasis on sustainability, with Fair Trade, organic, and carbon-neutral initiatives leading the way toward a more ethical and eco-friendly coffee industry.

Encouragement to Reflect

As you close this book, it's time to reflect on your own coffee habits. Coffee is an experience that's deeply personal—each cup is as unique as the person who drinks it. Whether you savor your coffee in peaceful solitude, share it with loved ones, or rely on it to power through the workday, the role it plays in your life is undoubtedly significant.

Think about how coffee fits into your daily routine. Do you start the day with a comforting cup at home, or do you grab a latte on your commute? Do you use coffee as a way to take a break, connect with coworkers, or spark creativity? As we've seen, the impact of coffee goes beyond its immediate effects on alertness and focus—it's a social ritual, a cultural symbol, and an essential part of modern life.

As coffee culture continues to evolve, so too will the ways we engage with it. New trends, technologies, and sustainability efforts will shape the future of coffee, offering even more ways for us to enjoy and appreciate this beloved drink. By making conscious choices about the coffee we consume—whether it's selecting ethically sourced beans, supporting local cafés, or choosing reusable cups—we can help ensure that coffee remains a force for good in both our personal lives and the world around us.

In the end, coffee is more than just a drink; it's a reflection of who we are, how we connect, and how we navigate the world. Whether you're a casual coffee drinker or a dedicated enthusiast, I hope this book has deepened your understanding and appreciation of the role coffee plays in daily life.

So, as you enjoy your next cup of coffee, take a moment to reflect. Savor the taste, the aroma, and the ritual. And remember that each cup of coffee is an opportunity—to connect, to focus, to relax, and to enjoy the simple pleasures of life.

Notes:

Notes:

Notes:

Notes:

Notes:

Notes:

Notes:

Notes:

www.ingramcontent.com/pod-product-compliance
Lightning Source LLC
Chambersburg PA
CBHW070348230526
45471CB00006B/2466